PREFACE

We are delighted to present this comprehensive collection of CBSE Data Science Class 12 Unsolved Papers for the academic years 2023 and 2024, compiled under subject code 844. This book is designed as a vital resource for students preparing for their board examinations, providing them with an authentic and challenging set of practice papers directly sourced from the CBSE board exams.

The field of Data Science is both dynamic and demanding, requiring a deep understanding of theoretical concepts as well as practical applications. These unsolved papers offer students the opportunity to practice and refine their problem-solving skills, allowing them to assess their readiness and identify areas where further study is needed.

Key Features of the Book:

Authentic Exam Papers: This book includes the actual question papers from the CBSE board exams of 2023 and 2024, ensuring that students are exposed to the most relevant and up-to-date material.

Real Exam Experience: By working through these unsolved papers, students can simulate the conditions of the actual exam, helping them build confidence and improve their time management skills.

Comprehensive Coverage: The papers cover all key topics within the Data Science syllabus, providing thorough practice across the subject.

Answer Writing Practice: The unsolved nature of the papers encourages students to develop their answer writing techniques, which is crucial for scoring high marks.

Critical Thinking and Problem Solving: These papers are designed to enhance students' critical thinking and problem-solving abilities by presenting a wide range of question types and complexities.

Perfect for Revision: This book serves as an ideal tool for last-minute revision, helping students to reinforce their knowledge and refine their exam strategies.

Self-Assessment and Improvement: Students can use these papers to self-assess their progress and identify areas where they need to focus more attention.

We believe that this book will be an invaluable resource for Class 12 students as they prepare for their Data Science board exams. By diligently working through these unsolved papers, students will not only improve their exam performance but also deepen their understanding of Data Science, laying a strong foundation for future studies and careers in this rapidly evolving field. We wish all students the best of luck in their exams and hope that this book serves as a crucial tool in their academic journey.

Table of Contents

CBSE Previous Year Question Paper 2023

SET-4

SUBJECT CODE: 844

Q.P. CODE: 368

Instructions:

Please check that this question paper contains **21** questions.

Q.P. Code given on the right-hand side of the question paper should be written on the title page of the answer-book by the candidate.

Please write down the serial number of the question in the answer-book before attempting it.

15-minute time has been allotted to read this question paper. The question paper will be distributed at 10.15 a.m. From 10.15 a.m. to 10.30 a.m., the students will read the question paper only and will not write any answer on the answer-book during this period.

DATA SCIENCE

Time allowed: 2 hours

Maximum Marks: 50

General Instructions:

1. Please read the instructions carefully.
2. This question paper consists of 21 questions in two sections: Section A and Section B.
3. Section A has Objective Type Questions, whereas Section B contains Subjective Type Questions.
4. Out of the given (5 + 16 =) 21 questions, the candidate has to answer (5 + 10 =) 15 questions in the allotted (maximum) time of 2 hours.
5. All questions of a particular section must be attempted in the correct order.
6. Section A: Objective Type Questions (24 marks):
    a. This section has 5 questions.
    b. There is no negative marking.

c. Do as per the instructions given.

d. Marks allotted are mentioned against each question/part.

7. Section B: Subjective Type Questions (26 marks):

a. This section has 16 questions.

b. A candidate has to do 10 questions.

c. Do as per the instructions given.

d. Marks allotted are mentioned against each question/part.

SECTION A

(Objective Type Questions) (24 marks)

1. Answer any 4 out of the given 6 questions on Employability Skills. (4 1=4)

(i) A/An may be defined as underlying characteristic of a person which results in effective and/or superior performance in a job.

(a) uncertainty

(b) competence

(c) obstacles

(d) fear

(ii) Which of the following is not true for formulas in a spreadsheet?

(a) A formula always starts with an equal to (=) sign.

(b) A formula is displayed in the formula bar.

(c) Formulae are used to calculate results through arithmetic operations.

(d) In numeric formulae, you cannot make use of operators.

(iii) Given below are two statements, one labelled as Assertion (A) and the other labelled as Reason (R). Select the correct answer from the

(iv) code given below:

Assertion (A): Physiological motivation can be guided by the need for achievement and the need for affiliation.

Reason (R): The need for achievement is a social form of motivation involving a competitive drive to meet the standards of excellence.

Code:

(a) Both Assertion (A) and Reason (R) are true and Reason (R) is the correct explanation of

Assertion (A).

(b) Both Assertion (A) and Reason (R) are true, but Reason (R) is not the correct explanation of Assertion (A).

(c) Assertion (A) is true, but Reason (R) is false.

(d) Assertion (A) is false, but Reason (R) is true.

(v) If the column is not wide enough to display the value, which of the following errors is displayed?

(a) #VALUE!

(b) #DIV/0!

(c) #####

(d) #COLUMN!

(vi) Which term is used to describe a person's ability to recognize what results are important and the steps needed to be taken to achieve them?

(a) Motivation

(b) Result Orientation

(c) Stress Management

(d) Goal Setting

(vii) Given below are two statements, one labelled as Assertion (A) and the other labelled as Reason (R). Select the correct answer from the code given below:

Assertion (A): Many entrepreneurs are not considered experts in their line of business, but still they make important decisions and solve issues everyday within their industry.

Reason (R): By preparing oneself to take on the challenge and by taking smaller steps to work towards it, fearful situations can also start to feel comfortable.

Code:

(a) Both Assertion (A) and Reason (R) are true and Reason (R) is the correct explanation of Assertion (A).

(b) Both Assertion (A) and Reason (R) are true, but Reason (R) is not the correct explanation of Assertion (A).

(c) Assertion (A) is true, but Reason (R) is false.

(d) Assertion (A) is false, but Reason (R) is true.

2. Answer any 5 out of the given 6 questions. (5 1=5)

(i) is the right of an individual to have control over how his or her personal information is collected and used.

(a) Data Privacy

(b) Data Governance

(c) Governing

(d) Data Quality

(ii) Which of the following refers to the process of identifying incorrect, incomplete and inaccurate data?

(a) Exploratory Data Analysis

(b) Data Cleaning

(c) Univariate Analysis

(d) Data Ethics

(iii) Every _____________represents the outcome of the test in a decision tree.

(a) Internal node

(b) External node

(c) Branch

(d) Leaf node

(iv) The algorithm is one of the most basic and easy-to-implement supervised machine learning algorithms.

(a) Decision tree

(b) K-nearest neighbors (K-NN)

(c) Classification

(d) Scoping

(v) ____ is the square root of the variance of the residuals.

(a) Root Mean Square Deviation

(b) Required Mean Similar Deviation

(c) Root Median Similar Deviation

(d) Regular Mean Square Deviation

(vi) In which type of learning do algorithms act on data without human intervention?

(a) Unsupervised

(b) Supervised

(c) Limited

(d) Conditional

3. Answer any 5 out of the given 6 questions. (5 1=5)

(i)PDP stands for

(a) Personal Data Protection Bill

(b) Private Data Protection Bill

(c) Personal Device Protection Bill

(d) Personal Device Prevention Bill

(ii) ______ is a more complex form of statistical analysis technique and is used to analyze more than two variables in the data set.

(a) Graphical method

(b) Multivariate analysis

(c) Univariate analysis

(d) Unsupervised learning technique

(iii) Decision trees are used to solve problems.

(a) Only classification

(b) Only regression

(c) Both classification and regression

(d) All universal

(iv) Can we use K-NN algorithms for data mining problems?

(v) Y = m X + b is the formula for __________.

(a) Mean Absolute Error

(b) Root Mean Square Deviation

(c) Simple linear regression

(d) Simple linear classification

(vi) State whether the following statement is true or false:

The formula for non-linear and linear regression is same.

4. Answer any 5 out of the given 6 questions. (5 1=5)

(i) The Children's Online Privacy and Protection Act is a law that deals with

(a) privacy policy for children who are less than the age of 13 years.

(b) privacy policy for adults.

(c) public policy for all children.

(d) protection policy for mothers of newborns.

(ii) The process of Exploratory Data Analysis is done with the help of summary statistics and representations.

(a) Analytical

(b) Graphical

(c) Logical

(d) Sequential

(iii) Regression trees are used when the dependent variable is non-continuous. Is the given statement true or false?

(iv) Which of the following is true for K-NN algorithm?

(a) Interpretability of the K-NN algorithm is very low.

(b) The K-NN algorithm explicitly has a training step.

(c) The K-NN algorithm is not sensitive to outliers.

(d) K-NN works well with a small number of input variables, but as the number of variables grow, the K-NN algorithm struggles to predict the output of a new data point.

(v) The actual value of the depends on the data and accuracy required.

(a) RMSE

(b) MAE

(c) NLR

(d) model

(vi) Trigonometric functions are examples of linear functions.

Is the given statement true or false?

5. Answer any 5 out of the given 6 questions. (5 1=5)

(i) Ethics govern the behaviour or actions of an individual.

(a) True

(b) False

(ii) Bivariate analysis is also a good way to measure the between the two variables.

(a) Difference

(b) Mean

(c) Correlation

(d) Median

(iii) For every possible decision in a decision tree, stemming from the root makes a _________.

(a) Branch

(b) Tree

(c) Root

(d) Node

(iv) __________is a non-parametric algorithm, as it does not assume anything about the distribution of the data.

(a) Cross Validation

(b) Regression

(c) Dataset

(d) K-NN

(v) What is the basic objective of linear regression?

(a) To reduce the distance between the line and data points to make it minimum.

(b) To increase the distance between the line and data points to make it maximum.

(c) To find the sum of the distance between the line and data points.

(d) To find the average of the distance between the line and data points.

(vi) A _________ regression equation has an intercept on the right-hand side and an explanatory variable with a coefficient.

(a) circular

(b) multiple

(c) complex

(d) simple

SECTION B

(Subjective Type Questions) (26 marks)

Answer any 3 out of the given 5 questions on Employability Skills. Answer each question in 20 30 words. (3 2=6)

6. List any two benefits of Entrepreneurial Competencies.
7. Answer the following questions from the spreadsheet given below:

My Store				
	A	B	C	D
1	**Product**	**Cost Price**	**Selling Price**	**Profit/Loss**
2	Ruler	9	15	
3	Crayons	23	25	
4	Pens	14	12	
5	Cardboard	35	45	
6	Highest			

a. Write a formula in cell D2, to calculate the Profit or Loss for the item 'Ruler' as the difference of "Cost Price" and "Selling Price".

b. Write a function in B6 to display the highest cost price of the product.

8. List any two sources of motivation and inspiration.

9. Differentiate between internal and external motivation. Give a suitable example.

10. Match the given attitudes of an entrepreneur with their characteristics:

Attitudes	Characteristics
a) Interpersonal skills	(i) Ability to take charge and act in a (ii) situation before others
b) Taking initiative	(iii) Ability to continue to do something even when it is difficult.
c) Decisiveness	(iv) Ability to work with others
d) Perseverance	(v) Ability to make quick and profitable

Answer any 4 out of the given 6 questions in 20 - 30 words each. (4 2=8)

11. Name the areas of focus of data governance.

12. Differentiate between Univariate analysis and Bivariate analysis.

13. Why are decision trees considered to be versatile?

14. What is the principle on which K-NN algorithm work2

15. When do we use linear regression?

16. The formula for non-linear regression is y ~ f (x, β).

What do x and y denote in the given formula?

Answer any 3 out of the given 5 questions in 50 - 80 words each. (3 4=12)

17. Write a short note on General Data Protection Regulation (GDPR).

18. List any four tools and methods used to perform Exploratory Analysis.

19. List any four important features of decision trees.

20. List any four disadvantages of K-NN compared to other algorithms.

21. Explain in points the working of 'k-means clustering algorithm'

CBSE Previous Year Question Paper 2024

SET-4

SUBJECT CODE: 844

Q.P. CODE: 368

Instructions:

Please check that this question paper contains **21** questions.

Q.P. Code given on the right-hand side of the question paper should be written on the title page of the answer-book by the candidate.

Please write down the serial number of the question in the answer-book before attempting it.

15-minute time has been allotted to read this question paper. The question paper will be distributed at 10.15 a.m. From 10.15 a.m. to 10.30 a.m., the students will read the question paper only and will not write any answer on the answer-book during this period.

DATA SCIENCE

Time allowed: 2 hours

Maximum Marks: 50

General Instructions:

1. Please read the instructions carefully.
2. This question paper consists of 21 questions in two sections: Section A and Section B.
3. Section A has Objective Type Questions, whereas Section B contains Subjective Type Questions.
4. Out of the given (5 + 16 =) 21 questions, the candidate has to answer (5 + 10 =) 15 questions in the allotted (maximum) time of 2 hours.
5. All questions of a particular section must be attempted in the correct order.
6. Section A: Objective Type Questions (24 marks):
    a. This section has 5 questions.
    b. There is no negative marking.

c. Do as per the instructions given.

d. Marks allotted are mentioned against each question/part.

7. Section B: Subjective Type Questions (26 marks):

a. This section has 16 questions.

b. A candidate has to do 10 questions.

c. Do as per the instructions given.

d. Marks allotted are mentioned against each question/part.

SECTION A

(Objective Type Questions) (24 marks)

1. Answer any 4 out of the given 6 questions on Employability Skills. (4 1=4)

(i) Match the following personalities with their parameters, based on Five Factor Model.

a. Extraversion -(i) Self-disciplined and take care of others before themselves.

b. Neuroticism - (ii) Talkative, confident and make any gathering lively.

c. Consciousness - (iii) Self-doubt, depression and shyness.

(a) a- (ii), b - (iii), c- (i)

(b) a- (i), b- (ii), c- (iii)

(c) a- (iii), b- (ii), c- (i)

(d) a- (ii), b- (i), c- (iii)

(ii) A _________ is a company that is in the first stage of its operations.

(a) Corporation

(b) Startup

(c) Multinational

(d) Conglomerate

(iii) Which non-verbal cue is not associated with active listening?

(a) Nodding in agreement

(b) Maintaining an open and welcoming body posture

(c) Checking your phone when the other person is speaking

(d) Making encouraging facial expressions

(iv) Statement (A): To sum the values in cells A1 through A10 in a spreadsheet, the formula used is "=SUM (A1:A10)".

Statement (A): To sum the values in cells A1 through A10 in a spreadsheet, the formula used is "=SUM (A1:A10)".

(a) Both (A) and (B) are true.

(b) Both (A) and (B) are false.

(c) (A) is true, but (B) is false.

(d) (A) is false, but (B) is true.

(v) Why is setting SMART goals important in self-management?

(a) It makes goals too rigid.

(b) It allows for vague and undefined goals.

(c) It defines action-based steps that one will follow to achieve the goal.

(d) It discourages goal setting altogether.

(vi) Which of the following is a benefit of green jobs?

(a) They do not support adaptation to climate change.

(b) They control waste and pollution.

(c) They increase greenhouse gas emissions.

(d) They decrease efficiency of raw materials.

2. Answer any 5 out of the given 6 questions. **(5X1=5)**

(i) EDA stands for:

(a) Exploratory Data Analysis

(b) Efficient Data Accumulation

(c) Extended Data Assessment

(d) Essential Data Application

(ii) Assertion (A): Decision trees are versatile algorithms and are easy to visualize.

Reasoning (R): Decision trees can only be used to map linear relationships.

(a) Both (A) and (R) are true and (R) is correct explanation of (A).

(b) Both (A) and (R) are true and (R) is not correct explanation of (A).

(c) (A) is true and (R) is false.

(d) (R) is true and (A) is false.

(iii) Which of the following is not a focus area of data governance?

(a) Data integrity

(b) Data availability

(c) Usability of data

(d) Data visualization

(iv) In the K-Nearest Neighbors (KNN) algorithm, what does the "K" represent?

(a) K is the number of training examples.

(b) K is the number of points that the K-NN algorithm checks before doing a majority vote.

(c) K is the number of points that the K-NN algorithm checks before doing a minority vote.

(d) K is the dimensionality of the data.

(v) Regression methods that do not have a linear function are called:

(a) Linear regression models

(b) Non-linear regression models

(c) Exponential regression models

(d) Polynomial regression models

(vi) What is the primary characteristic of Multiple Linear Regression?

(a) It uses only one independent variable to predict the outcome of a dependent variable.

(b) It uses multiple dependent variables to predict the outcome of a single independent variable.

(c) It uses multiple independent variables to predict the outcome of a dependent variable.

(d) It employs categorical variables exclusively for prediction.

3. Answer any 5 out of the given 6 questions. **(5X1=5)**

(i) True or False: A company is collecting and storing personal identifiable information in a secure, encrypted format without obtaining explicit consent from the user. There is no agreement from the user regarding the collection of the data by the company. It is a clear violation of data privacy rules.

(ii) Statistical methods like mean, mode, median, range, variance and standard deviation are used for:

(a) Bivariate Analysis

(b) Multivariate Analysis

(c) Univariate Analysis

(d) Exponential Analysis

(iii) When using a decision tree for classification, what does each leaf node represent?

(a) A subset of the dataset

(b) A class label

(c) A threshold value

(d) A continuous variable

(iv) What is the curse of dimensionality in the context of the K-Nearest Neighbors (KNN) algorithm?

(a) It refers to the phenomenon where KNN works well with a large number of input variables.

(b) It describes the ease with which KNN handles high- dimensional data.

(c) It suggests that KNN is not affected by the number of input variables.

(d) It explains that KNN works well with a small number of input variables but struggles as the number of variables grows.

(v) The diagram below shows a scatter plot of two variables X and Y. Linear regression helps us to find Line X. What is Line X known as?

(a) Correlation line

(b) Line of best fit

(c) Regression line

(d) Trend line

(vi) What problem-solving approach does the K-Means clustering algorithm use?

(a) Gradient Descent

(b) Expectation-Maximization

(c) Principal Component Analysis (PCA)

(d) Genetic Algorithm

4. Answer any 5 out of the given 6 questions. **(5X1=5)**

(i) The European Union made protect European Union consumer data. effective on May 25th, 2018 to protect European Union consumer data.

(a) Health Insurance Portability and Accountability Act

(b) General Data Protection Regulation

(c) Personal Data Protection Bill

(d) California Consumer Privacy Act

(ii) In a market survey we are analyzing the relationship between price and sales of a product to see if there is any relationship. This kind of analysis is a/an:

(a) Descriptive Analysis

(b) Univariate Analysis

(c) Multivariate Analysis

(d) Bivariate Analysis

(iii) What is the value of the terminal nodes in a regression tree after training?

(a) The minimum of the observations

(b) The maximum of the observations

(c) The mode of the observations

(d) The mean of the observations

(iv) Why is the K-Nearest Neighbors (KNN) algorithm very sensitive to outliers?

(a) KNN relies on a fixed value of K, which makes it prone to outliers.

(b) KNN does not consider the distances between data points.

(c) KNN chooses neighbors based on distance criteria, and outliers can significantly affect distance calculations.

(d) KNN only works with categorical data, and outliers are more common in continuous data.

(v) In real-life scenarios, why is it typically best to have a small Root Mean Squared Error (RMSE) value in regression models?

(a) A small RMSE indicates a higher Mean Absolute Error.

(b) A small RMSE indicates a stronger linear relationship between dependent and independent variables.

(c) A small RMSE signifies higher accuracy of the model's predictions.

(d) A small RMSE suggests that the model needs to be retrained.

(vi) State True or False.

Clustering techniques apply when instances of data are to be divided into natural groups.

5. Answer any 5 out of the given 6 questions. (5X1=5)

(i) Statement 1: At any point of time, an individual can request an organization to remove all the data that they have collected about him/her.

Statement 2: Data Privacy is just about secure data storage.

(a) Both statement 1 and statement 2 are correct.

(b) Both statement 1 and statement 2 are incorrect.

(c) Statement 1 is correct and statement 2 is incorrect.

(d) Statement 2 is correct and statement 1 is incorrect.

(ii) Identify the correct match.

A. Supervised Learning - (i) Uses non-classified data

B. Unsupervised Learning - (ii) Clustering method

C. K-Means - (iii) Uses well labelled data

(a) a - (ii), b- (iii), c- (i)

(b) a- (i), b- (ii), c -(iii)

(c) a- (iii), b- (ii), c- (i)

(d) a- (ii), b- (i), c- (iii)

(iii) Which of the following is NOT an advantage of K-NN algorithm?

(a) No training step

(b) Sensitive to outliers

(c) Good for multi class problems

(d) No assumptions of data

(iv) Consider the following equation for Simple Linear Regression:

$$Y = m * X + b$$

(v) Which of the following is correct with respect to the given equation?

(a) Y is an independent variable and X is a dependent variable.

(b) Y is an intercept and X is a dependent variable.

(c) X is an intercept and Y is a dependent variable.

(d) Y is a dependent variable and X is an independent variable.

(vi) Which of the following is not Unsupervised Learning? a real-world application of

(a) Image segmentation for medical diagnosis

(b) Recommendation systems

(c) Natural language translation

(d) Anomaly detection in network security

(vii) The below mentioned formula represents:

$Y_i = \beta_0 + \beta_1 X_{i1} + \beta_2 X_{12} + \beta_3 X_{i3} + + \beta_p X_{ip} +$

Where i = 1, 2, 3, ... n for each observation.

(a) Linear Regression

(b) Non-Linear Regression

(c) Correlation

(d) Multiple Linear Regression

SECTION B

(Subjective Type Questions) (26 marks)

Answer any 3 out of the given 5 questions on Employability Skills. Answer each question in 20 - 30 words. (3X2=6)

6. Define the following terms:

(A) Social Entrepreneur

(B) First generation entrepreneurs

7. Identify the type of sentence used in the statement as declarative interrogative, exclamatory or imperative:

(A) Complete your work

(B) It's very yummy!

(C) Did you complete your homework?

(D) I received the prize for the best player in football team.

8. Why should a person adopt a positive attitude? Give any two reasons.

9. Following table shows marks of marks of 5 students of class IX in 3 subjects. Based on this data, calculate the following by writing a formula.

(A) Total marks of Rohit and Mudit in Sanskrit.

(B) Total marks of Avinash in 3 subjects.

10. Define Solid waste management. Mention any two specific areas within waste management where green jobs are prevalent.

Answer any 4 out of the given 6 questions in 20 30 words each. (4X2=8)

11. Explain the importance of data privacy in today's digital age and provide an example of a situation where a breach of data privacy could have significant consequences.

12. What are the two common techniques to handle missing data?

13. List any 2 advantages of using a decision tree.

14. Name and explain the two important characteristics of KNN.

15. Describe the purpose of the Mean Absolute Error (MAE) in Linear Regression.

16. Name any four clustering methods.

Answer any 3 out of the given 5 questions in 50-80 words each. (3X4=12)

17. Expand and explain COPPA.

18. Explain Univariate Analysis in detail. Give at least one example to support your answer.

19. Define a decision tree in the context of machine learning. Also, provide a labelled diagram of a simple decision tree.

20. Salma started a business 10 months back. It is observed that her income has increased exponentially every month.

(A) Which type of regression can you relate this to?

(B) Write the formula for part (A) and explain the terms used.

(C) What will be the shape of graph formed in this case?

21. Explain the following:

(A) Unsupervised Learning

(B) K-means Clustering

CBSE Previous Year Question Paper 2025

SET-4

SUBJECT CODE: 844

Q.P. CODE: 368

Instructions:

Please check that this question paper contains **21** questions.

Q.P. Code given on the right-hand side of the question paper should be written on the title page of the answer-book by the candidate.

Please write down the serial number of the question in the answer-book before attempting it.

15-minute time has been allotted to read this question paper. The question paper will be distributed at 10.15 a.m. From 10.15 a.m. to 10.30 a.m., the students will read the question paper only and will not write any answer on the answer-book during this period.

DATA SCIENCE

Time allowed: 2 hours

Maximum Marks: 50

General Instructions:

1. Please read the instructions carefully.
2. This question paper consists of 21 questions in two sections: Section A and Section B.
3. Section A has Objective Type Questions, whereas Section B contains Subjective Type Questions.
4. Out of the given (5 + 16 =) 21 questions, the candidate has to answer (5 + 10 =) 15 questions in the allotted (maximum) time of 2 hours.
5. All questions of a particular section must be attempted in the correct order.
6. Section A: Objective Type Questions (24 marks):
    a. This section has 5 questions.
    b. There is no negative marking.

c. Do as per the instructions given.

d. Marks allotted are mentioned against each question/part.

7. Section B: Subjective Type Questions (26 marks):

a. This section has 16 questions.

b. A candidate has to do 10 questions.

c. Do as per the instructions given.

d. Marks allotted are mentioned against each question/part.

Section – A
(Objective Type Questions)

1. Answer any 4 out of the given 6 questions on Employability Skills. (4 X 1 = 4)

(i) With reference to describing an individual's personality, FFM stands for :
(A) Flexible Framework Model
(B) Functional Flexibility Model
(C) Focused Feedback Method
(D) Five Factor Model

(ii) Which of the following is a barrier that entrepreneurs may face while running their ventures ?
(A) Availability of skilled labours
(B) Self-confidence
(C) Unavailability of monetary resources on time
(D) Risk taking capability

(iii) Identify the active voice sentence from the following :
(A) The game was won by the home team.
(B) The report is being written by the manager.
(C) The manager is writing the report.
(D) The homework was done by the student.

(iv) The shortcut key to add a new slide in a presentation is :
(A) Ctrl + N
(B) Ctrl + Alt + N
(C) Ctrl + M
(D) Ctrl + Alt + M

(v) Which term is used for motivation that comes from within an individual rather than external rewards ?
(A) Extrinsic motivation
(B) Increment motivation
(C) Intrinsic motivation
(D) Incentive-based motivation

(vi) With respect to green jobs, an Appropriate technology is the _________ technology that is environment friendly and suited to local needs.
(A) large-scale

(B) small-scale
(C) remote-scale

(D) old-scale

Answer any 5 out of the given 6 questions. (5 X 1 = 5)
(i) State whether the following statement is True or False :
In terms of data privacy, companies are considered the sole owners of user data.
(ii) The following histogram represents :

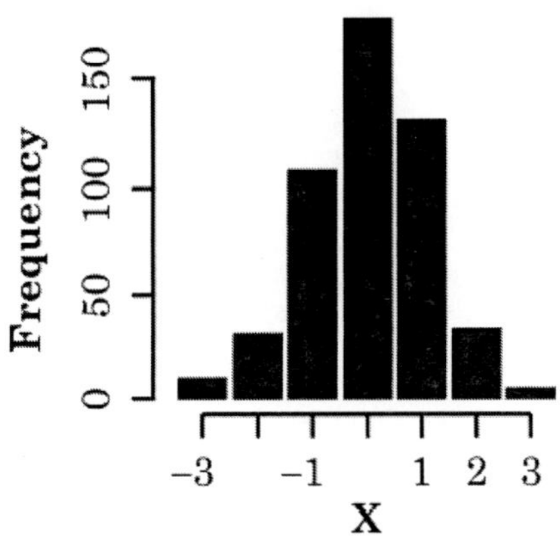

(A) Univariate Analysis
(B) Bivariate Analysis
(C) Multivariate Analysis
(D) Clustering
(iii) Name the algorithm which makes predictions based on the outcomes of several decision trees.
(A) Classification algorithm
(B) K-means clustering
(C) Random Forest algorithm
(D) K-nearest neighbour algorithm
(iv) Which characteristics describe K-Nearest Neighbours (K-NN) algorithm ?
(A) Lazy learning and parametric learning
(B) Eager learning and non-parametric learning
(C) Lazy learning and non-parametric learning
(D) Eager learning and parametric learning

Which type of analysis is suitable for examining the relationship between rainfall and crop growth and the amount of crop growth for a certain level of rainfall ?
(A) Classification
(B) Clustering
(C) Linear Regression
(D) Decision Tree
(vi) A website selling products uses recommendation engines to predict what products a customer is likely to purchase. This functionality is achieved through :
(A) Supervised Learning
(B) Unsupervised Learning
(C) Reinforcement Learning

(D) Natural Language Processing

3. Answer any 5 out of the given 6 questions. (5 X 1 = 5)

(i) CCPA stands for :
(A) California Consumer Privacy Act
(B) Children's Consumer Privacy Act
(C) California Consumer Public Act
(D) Children's Consumer Public Act

(ii) Which of the following are common techniques for handling missing data in a dataset ?
1. Remove the entire column of data.
2. Remove the row of data with missing values.
3. Insert a value close to the mean or mode of the variable with missing data.
4. Leave the missing data as it is.
5. Insert a random value.
(A) 1 and 2
(B) 2 and 3
(C) 3 and 4
(D) 4 and 5

In case of a classification tree, predictions on unseen data are made using the _________.
(A) Mean
(B) Median
(C) Mode
(D) RMSE

(iv) How does the curse of dimensionality affect the performance of the K-Nearest Neighbours (K-NN) algorithm ?
(A) K-NN performs better with an increasing number of input variables.
(B) K-NN struggles to predict the output accurately with an increasing number of input variables.
(C) K-NN becomes faster with more input variables due to increased computational power.
(D) K-NN becomes less sensitive to outliers with an increasing number of input variables.

(v) Assertion (A) : In real-life scenarios, a small RMSE value indicates a better model fit to the data and higher accuracy.
Reason (R) : A large RMSE value suggests that the model fits the data well.
(A) Both (A) and (R) are true, and (R) is the correct explanation of (A).
(B) Both (A) and (R) are true, but (R) is not the correct explanation of (A).
(C) (A) is true, but (R) is false.
(D) (A) is false, but (R) is true.

(vi) State if the following statement is True or False :
"Clustering Techniques apply when the instances are to be divided into natural groups."

Answer any 5 out of the given 6 questions. (5 X 1 = 5)

(i) Which of the following defines data privacy ?
(A) The right of individuals to control how their personal information is collected and used.
(B) The obligation of organisations to collect personal information for marketing purposes.

(C) The unrestricted sharing of personal information across platforms.
(D) The use of personal information without consent for research purposes.

(ii) Prediction of house prices in a city depends on factors such as the number of bedrooms, size of the house (square footage), location and age of the property. Which analysis technique is appropriate for this scenario ?
(A) Univariate
(B) Zerovariate
(C) Multivariate
(D) Both Univariate and Multivariate

(iii) Which fundamental principle does the K-Nearest Neighbours (K-NN) algorithm oparate on ?
(A) Objects that are similar tend to be located far apart.
(B) Objects that are similar tend to be located at random distances.
(C) Objects that are similar tend to be located in a scattered manner.
(D) Objects that are similar tend to be located close to each other.

(iv) Which type of variable does linear regression predict ?
(A) Categorical
(B) Discrete
(C) Continuous
(D) Binary

Consider the formula given below :
y ~ f(x, Y)
where x is a vector of independent variables and y is the dependent variable.
Identify the type of regression from the following.
(A) Linear Regression
(B) Non-Linear Regression
(C) Correlation Regression
(D) Multiple Linear Regression

(vi) What is a significant application of unsupervised learning in anomaly detection ?
(A) Identifying patterns in structured data
(B) Classifying data points into predefined categories
(C) Detecting unusual data points
(D) Predicting future outcomes

5. Answer any 5 out of the given 6 questions. (5 X 1 = 5)

(i) COPPA stands for _________ Online Privacy Protection Act.
(A) California's
(B) Children's
(C) Center's
(D) Channel's

(ii) Which statement correctly describes the use of regression and classification trees based on the nature of the dependent variable ?
(A) Regression trees are suitable for continuous dependent

variables, while classification trees are suitable for categorical dependent variables.
(B) Classification trees are suitable for continuous dependent variables, while regression trees are suitable for categorical dependent variables.
(C) Both regression and classification trees are suitable for continuous dependent variables.
(D) Both regression and classification trees are suitable for categorical dependent variables.

(iii) The following diagram represents :

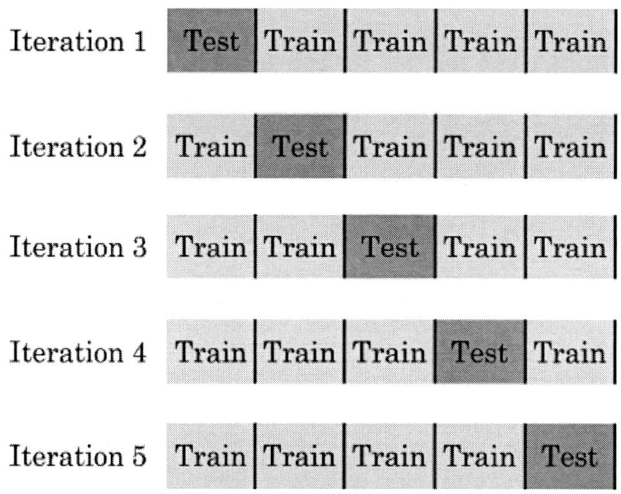

(A) Cross validation
(B) Regression
(C) Classification
(D) Neural Networks
(iv) When determining the line of best fit in linear regression, which method is used to minimize the deviation of the line from the actual data points ?
(A) Maximising the Sum of Squared Errors (SSE).
(B) Minimising the Mean Absolute Error (MAE).
(C) Using Principal Component Analysis (PCA).
(D) Optimising the F-statistic.
(v) The following graph represents :

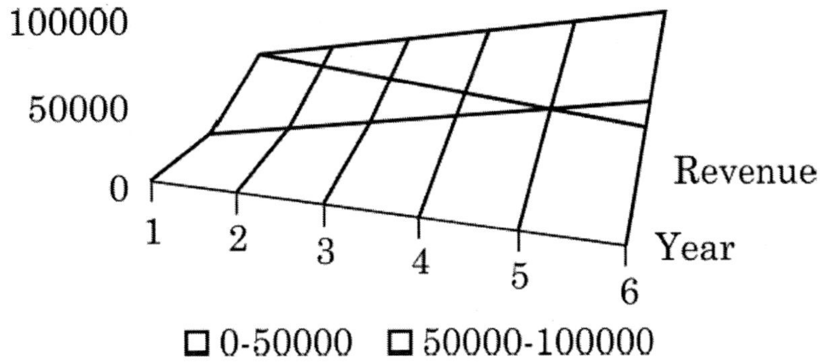

(A) Linear Regression (B) Multi-Linear Regression
(C) Classification (D) Correlation
(vi) Which problem-solving approach does the K-means algorithm employ ?
(A) Gradient Descent (B) Expectation-Maximisation
(C) Decision Trees (D) Support Vector Machines

Section – B
(Subjective Type Questions)

Answer any 3 out of the given 5 questions on Employability Skills in 20-30 words each. (3 X 2 = 6)

6. What are articles in a sentence ? Also give an example of a sentence exhibiting the usage of article.
7. Consider the following worksheet :

	A	B	C	D	E
1	S. No.	Item	Quantity	Price	Amount
2	1	Pen	10	60	
3	2	Glue stick	11	45	
4	3	Notebook	11	75	
5	4	Register	19	90	
6	5	Scale	5	5	

(a) In a spreadsheet, every formula starts with a/an _________ sign.
(b) Write the formula to calculate the amount for Glue-stick. (Amount is calculated as Price □ Quantity)
8. Identify and name the following personality disorders :
(a) A disorder characterised by intense self-doubt, a constant need for reassurance, dependency on others for decision-making, and avoidance of solitude.
(b) A disorder where individuals believe they are superior to others, lack empathy, and exaggerate their own achievements.
9. Discuss green jobs in transportation.
10. Discuss any two qualities of a successful entrepreneur.

Answer any 4 out of the given 6 questions in 20-30 words each. (4 X 2 = 8)

11. Explain two ethical guidelines relevant to software development and data management, emphasizing their importance in ensuring societal benefit and responsible use of technology.
12. Name one type of chart/graph suitable for analysing a single variable (univariate analysis) and one type for analyzing the relationship between two variables (bivariate analysis).
13. Explain cross-validation in data analysis.
14. Mention any two points of differentiation between Regression trees and Classification trees.
15. What is Root Mean Square Deviation ? Why it is used in data analysis ?
16. Text documents are often grouped based on their content similarity to efficiently organize and categorise them for information retrieval systems and recommendation engines. Identify and define the unsupervised learning method utilized in this context.

Answer any 3 out of the given 5 questions in 50-80 words each. (3 X 4 = 12)
17. Expand and explain PDP.
18. Explain Multivariate Analysis in detail. Give at least one example to support your answer.
19. List any four advantages of using a decision tree methodology.

20. Aarush started a business 6 months back. It has been noted that his income increases exponentially every month.
(a) Identify the appropriate regression model to illustrate Aarush's score trend.
(b) Write the formula/equation for the regression model.
(c) Draw a sample chart with dummy data depicting the above discussed regression model.
21. (a) Define the term clustering. Support your answer with a real life example.
(b) Name any two clustering methods.

ADDITIONAL RESOURCES

CLASS 12th Videos Playlist-

Link: https://www.youtube.com/playlist?list=PLzlh_31VWEFrZELIhMXtyH4vO8a5LIXi8

QR Code:

ADDITIONAL RESOURCES

Annual Test Papers Exam Practises

Sample Paper I
Link: https://forms.gle/6q73u8ir4Ei2iCeY6
QR Code:

Sample Paper II
Link: https://forms.gle/BkgT1HJ57kH3fu6o6
QR Code:

Sample Paper III
Link: https://forms.gle/4NfLDitGQqN4yeE48
QR Code:

Sample Paper IV
Link: https://forms.gle/Pxk6SyUCUiqxBHQZ7
QR Code:

YouTube Videos Playlists for all Chapters

Chapter 1
Link: https://www.youtube.com/playlist?list=PLzlh_31VWEFrBrzCa3K0n7qnpj7oVLXov
QR Code:

Chapter 2
Link:
https://www.youtube.com/playlist?list=PLzlh_31VWEFrCyQgcJSc1Fh2mRNnjTWqv
QR Code:

Chapter 3
Link:
https://www.youtube.com/playlist?list=PLzlh_31VWEFrCyQgcJSc1Fh2mRNnjTWqv
QR Code:

Chapter 4
Link:
https://www.youtube.com/playlist?list=PLzlh_31VWEFrGGQyh6MINX_pQnnC7z8hI
QR Code:

Chapter 5
Link: https://www.youtube.com/playlist?list=PLzlh_31VWEFoEKfyQj-wuzsrr53hbFhSN
QR Code:

Chapter 6
Link: https://www.youtube.com/playlist?list=PLzlh_31VWEFpoZifI01JAomqygcfKbUd4
QR Code:

Chapter 7
Link: https://www.youtube.com/playlist?list=PLzlh_31VWEFo5hygngcY6SnuA4pOx7jfB
QR Code:

Chapter 8
Link: https://www.youtube.com/playlist?list=PLzlh_31VWEFrJqsxSxq8Zpoj_DnJRDd9n
QR Code:

Chapter 9
Link: https://www.youtube.com/playlist?list=PLzlh_31VWEFoJcKFFNQq1Ye9d4lF8Qs4D

QR Code:

Chapter 10
Link: https://www.youtube.com/playlist?list=PLzlh_31VWEFq57uRBnqCtw2_lNaU6ettd
QR Code:

Chapter 11
Link: https://www.youtube.com/playlist?list=PLzlh_31VWEFplx3ZFuoo3Hx5hGP1GcgTo
QR Code:

Chapter 12
Link:
https://www.youtube.com/playlist?list=PLzlh_31VWEFrAXxOTvCUBExmWo0_91dVV
QR Code:

Chapter 13
Link: https://www.youtube.com/playlist?list=PLzlh_31VWEFosYeGlaXOpPC4t4EDdaI1G
QR Code:

9 789369 729579

Printed at Repro India Ltd.